Solar System Explorers

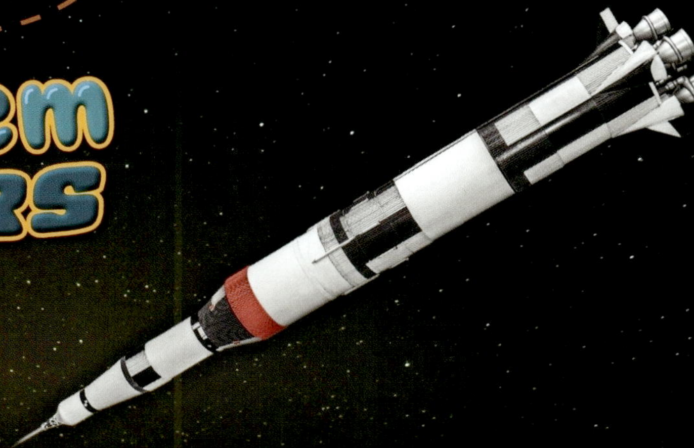

Venus

Written by
E.C. Andrews

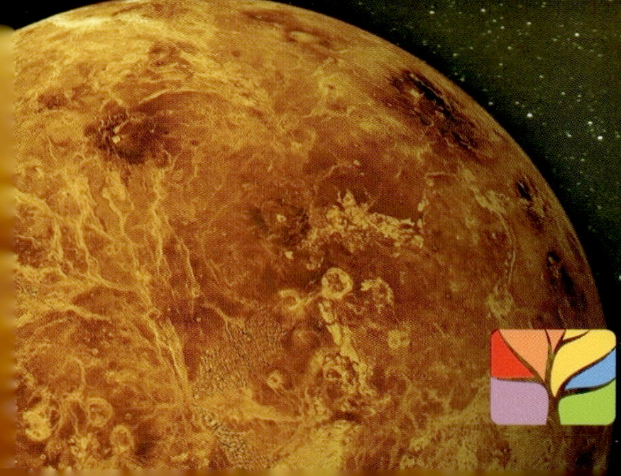

KidHaven
PUBLISHING

Published in 2026 by
KidHaven Publishing, an Imprint of
Greenhaven Publishing, LLC
2544 Clinton St., Buffalo, NY 14224

Written by: E.C. Andrews
Edited by: Noah Leatherland
Designed by: Amelia Harris

Cataloging-in-Publication Data
Names: Andrews, E.C.
Title: Venus / E.C. Andrews.
Description: Buffalo, NY : Kidhaven Publishing, 2026. | Series: Solar System Explorers | Includes glossary and index
Identifiers: ISBN 9781534549944 (pbk) | ISBN 9781534549951 (library bound) | ISBN 9781534549968 (ebook)
Subjects: LCSH: Venus (Planet)—Juvenile Literature
Classification: LCC QB681 A53 2026 | DDC 523.47--dc25

Manufactured in the United States of America

CPSIA compliance information: Batch #CSKH26
For further information contact Greenhaven Publishing LLC at 1-844-317-7404.

Please visit our website, www.greenhavenpublishing.com.
For a free color catalog of all our high-quality books, call toll free 1-844-317-7404 or fax 1-844-317-7405.

Find us on

Image Credits

Images are courtesy of Shutterstock.com. With thanks to Getty Images, Thinkstock Photo and iStockphoto. Cover – 19 STUDIO, AspctStyle, andreysharonov, leshiy985. Recurring Images – thomas eder, YummyBuum, Sabelskaya. 4–5 – Withan Tor, 24K-Production, 6–7 – MattL_Images, Johan Swanepoel. 8–9 – Vadim Sadovski, Artsiom P. 10–11 – AspctStyle. 12–13 – Artsiom P, Vadim Sadovski. 14–15 – NASA images, Artsiom P. 16–17 – Artsiom P. 18–19 – muratart, Dima Zel, Mopic. 20–21 – Artsiom P, NASA/JPL, Public domain, via Wikimedia Commons. 22–23 – 19 STUDIO, Aphelleon.

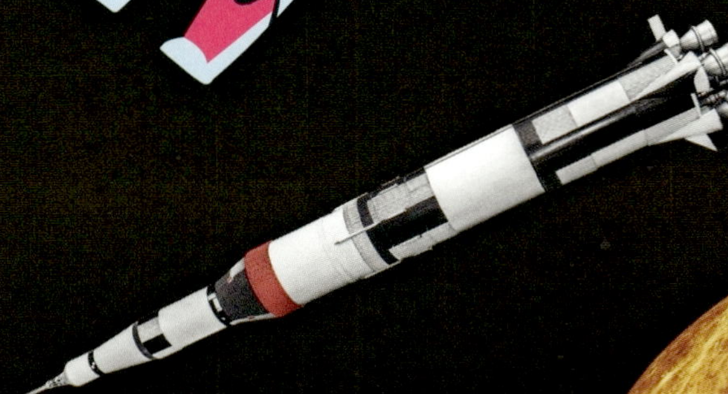

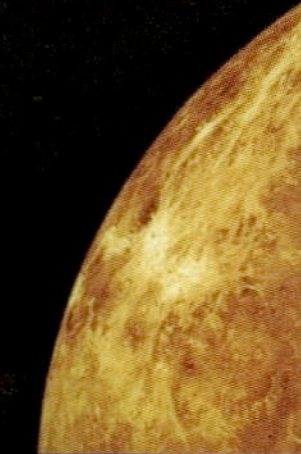

Contents

Words that look like **this** can be found in the glossary on page 24.

Let's Explore!

The solar system has eight planets, five dwarf planets, and hundreds of moons.

The solar system is a collection of planets and other objects. They all **orbit** around a star called the sun. Have you ever wondered what it might be like to explore the solar system?

Well, hop aboard our spaceship because we are blasting off to a new mission. I hope you have got your special spacesuit on. You are going to need it where we are going.

Where Is Venus?

Each planet is a different distance away from the sun. If we were to line the planets up in order of distance from the sun, it would look a bit like this:

Venus is about 67 million miles (108 million km) away from the sun. That may sound like a long way, but it is actually the second closest planet to the sun. The closest is Mercury.

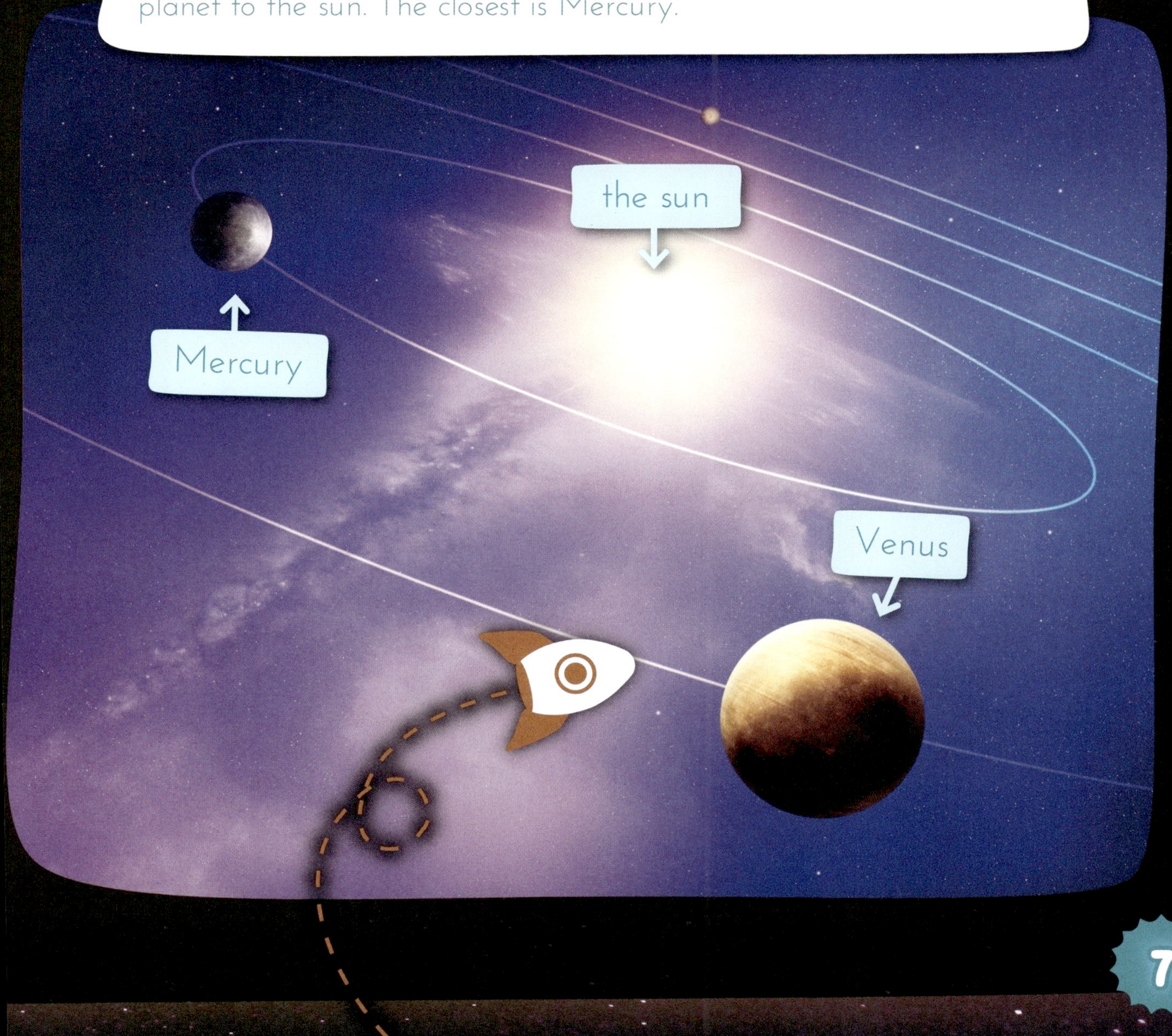

Round and Round

It takes Earth around 365 days to orbit the sun. This is how humans measure one year. It takes Venus 225 days to orbit the sun.

Venus takes less time to orbit the sun than Earth because it is closer.

As planets orbit, they spin on an **axis**. It takes Earth about 24 hours to spin around once. This is how we measure a day. However, Venus takes 5,832 hours to complete one spin.

Planet Profile

I have made some notes on Venus in the explorer's database. Let's take a look!

Temperature

Water freezes at 32 degrees Fahrenheit (0°C).

Size

- Around: 23,600 miles (38,000 km)
- Across: 7,500 miles (12,000 km)

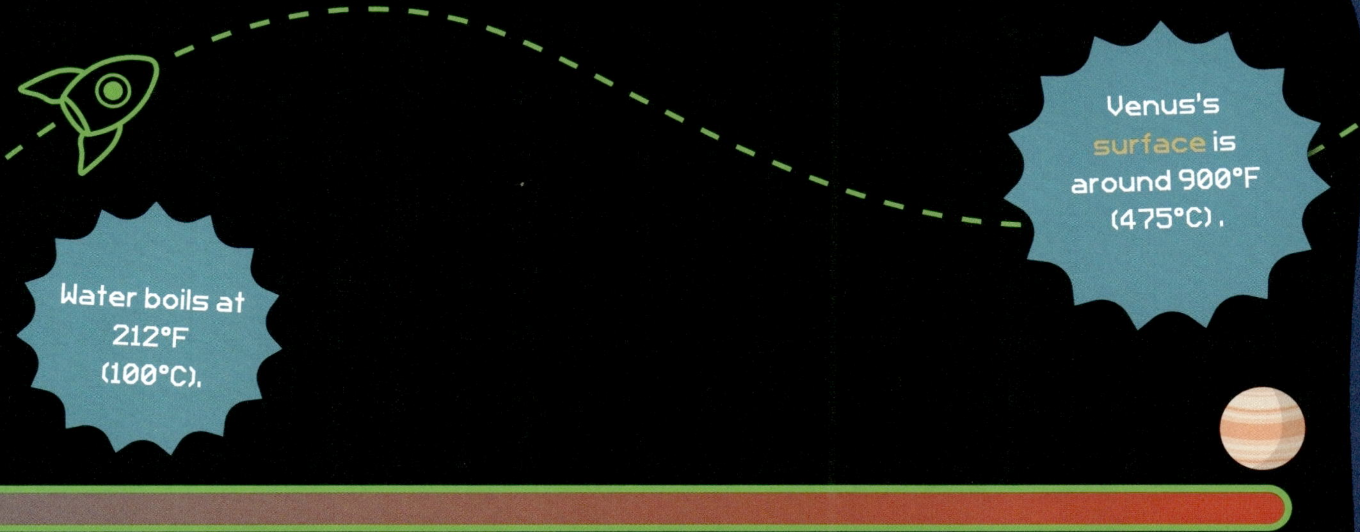

What Is Venus Made Of?

Venus is a rocky planet. Rocky planets have hard surfaces. They are mostly made up of rocks and different types of metals. Much of Venus's surface is covered by mountains and **volcanoes**.

surface of Venus

Venus is thought to have three main layers.

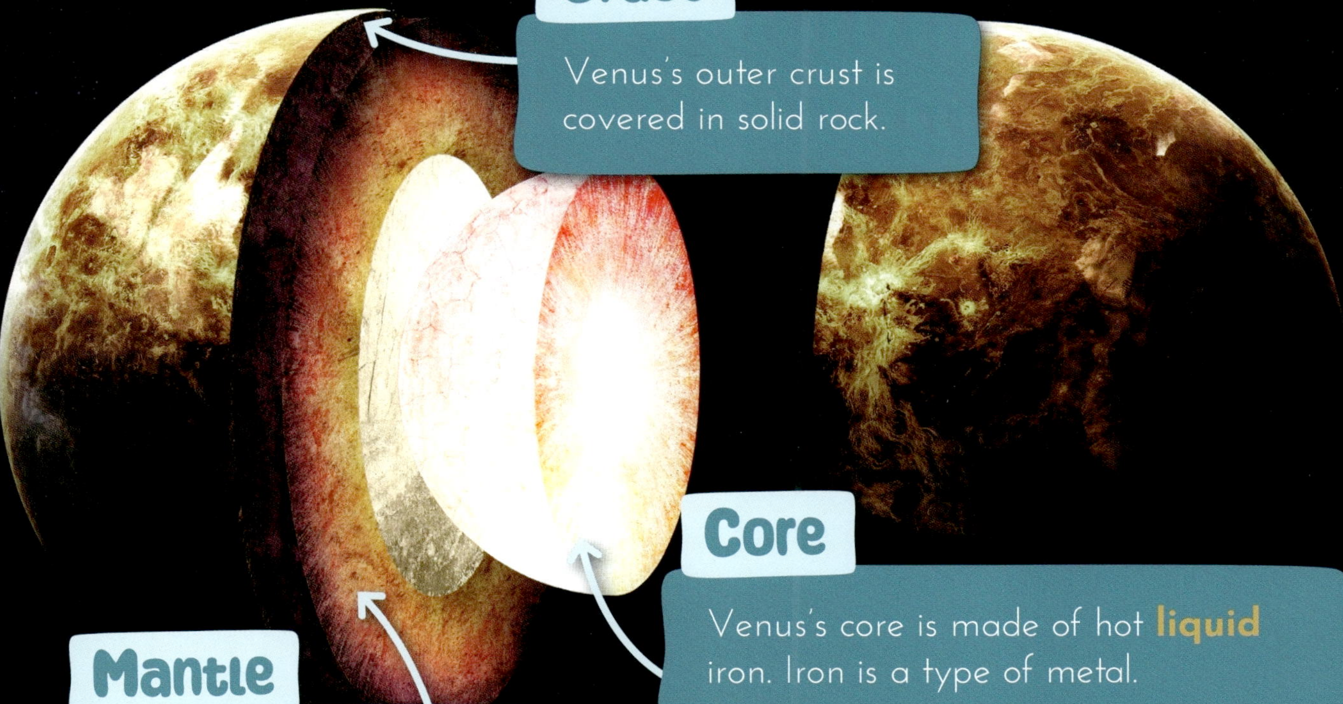

Watching the Weather

Around Venus, there is a layer of air called the atmosphere. The atmosphere around Venus is made of **gases** that trap heat from the sun. This makes Venus the hottest planet in the solar system.

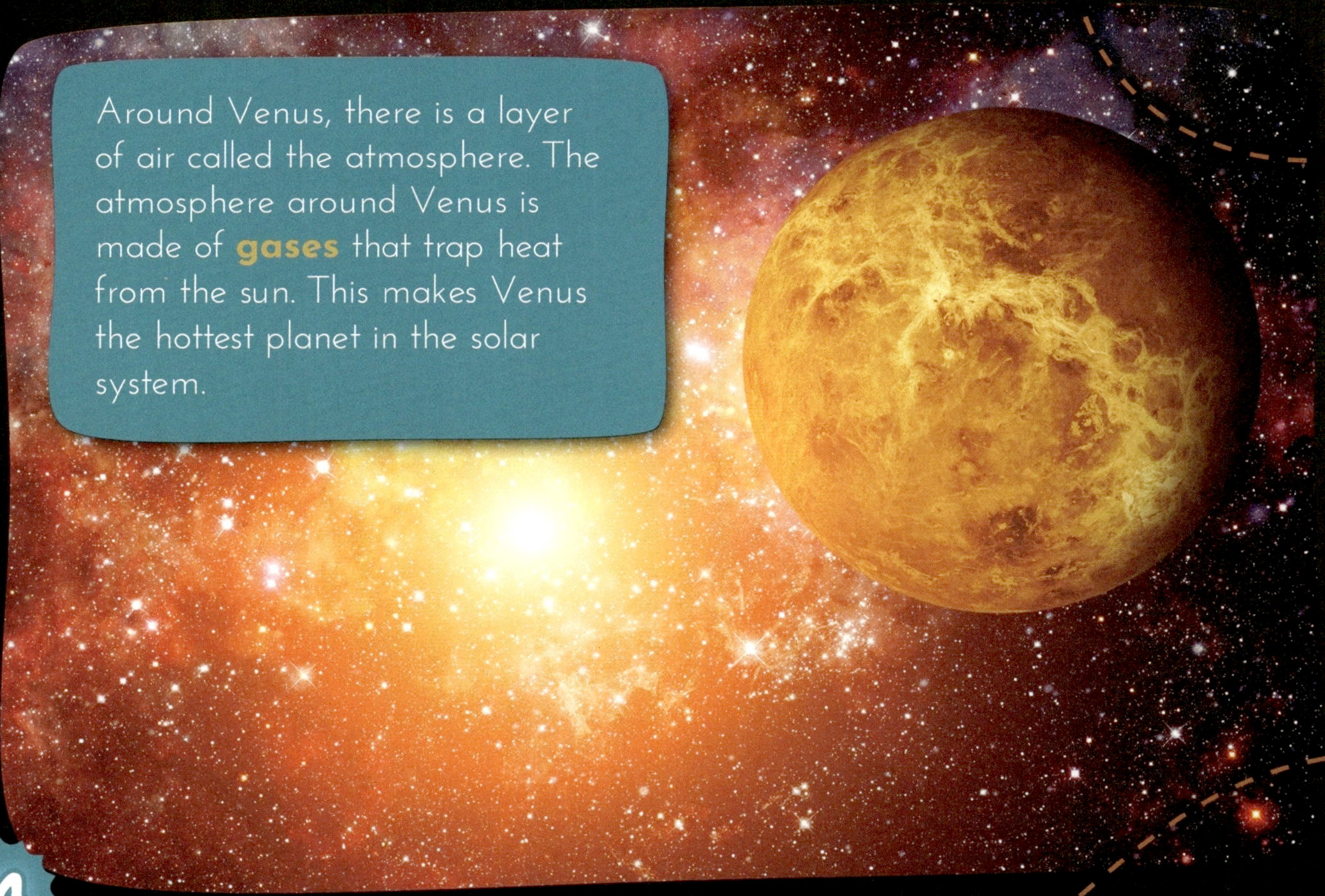

The weather on Venus is very hot, dry, and windy. The clouds on Venus are made of sulphuric acid, which falls as acid rain. This would be very dangerous to humans. It can burn through clothes and skin.

Is There Life on Venus?

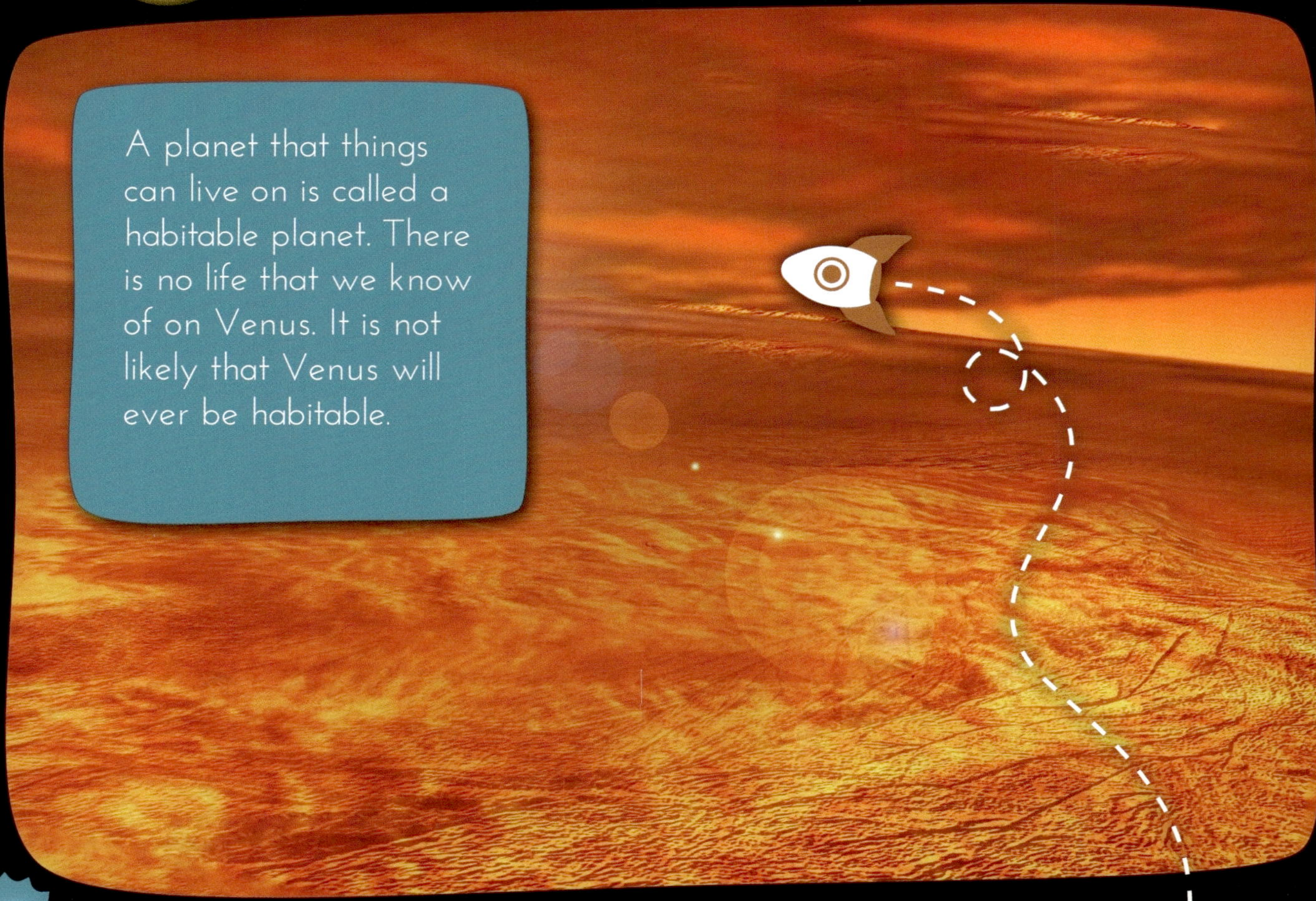

A planet that things can live on is called a habitable planet. There is no life that we know of on Venus. It is not likely that Venus will ever be habitable.

Firstly, the surface of Venus is far too hot for anything to survive. Without special spacesuits, we would melt! The atmosphere is also made of very poisonous gases.

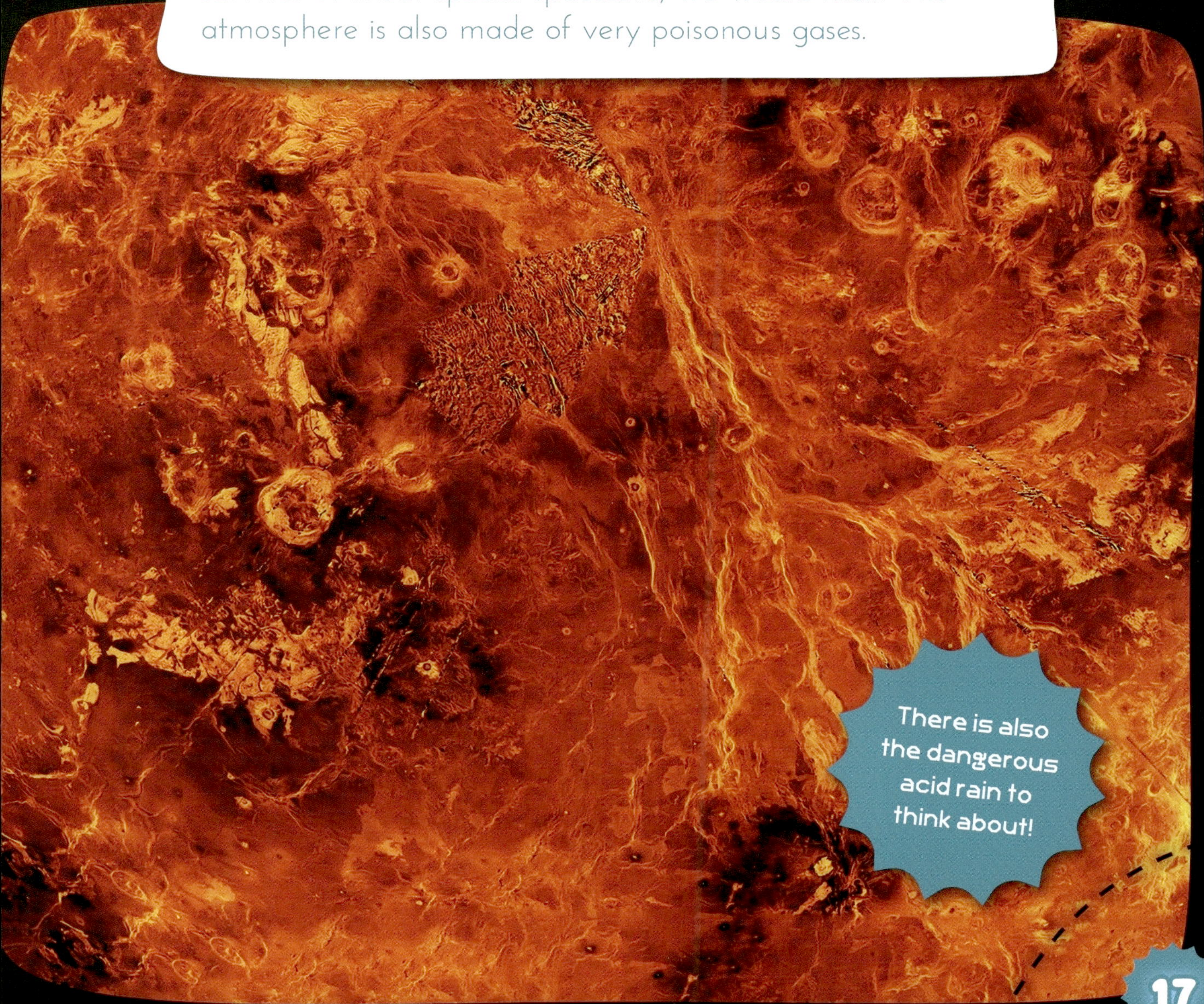

There is also the dangerous acid rain to think about!

Spot the Satellites

Something that orbits a bigger object in space is called a satellite. Some satellites are **natural**. Natural satellites are often made of rocks. However, some satellites are made by humans.

Moons are natural satellites.

Earth's moon

human-made satellite

Venus does not have any natural satellites. However, Venus has something called a quasi-satellite. Quasi-satellites orbit the sun and also move around a planet. Venus's quasi-satellite is called Zoozve.

Zoozve is an asteroid. An asteroid is a rocky object that orbits the sun.

Mega Mountains

The surface of Venus is covered in mountains and volcanoes. The volcanoes on Venus are some of the largest in the entire solar system. Large parts of Venus are covered in **lava**.

The tallest mountains on Venus are called the Maxwell Montes. They are in a place called Ishtar Terra. Some of the mountains in Ishtar Terra are around 7 miles (11 km) high.

More to Explore

What an adventure we have had on Venus. We have learned so many amazing things about this scary but incredible planet. It is a good thing we had our special spacesuits!

For now, though, we can leave our sunhats and acid-proof umbrellas behind because it is time to move on. There are many more planets waiting to be explored!

Glossary

axis	an imaginary line that something turns on
degrees	measuring units used to explain how hot or cold something is
gases	things that are like air, which fill any space available
lava	very hot melted rock
liquid	a material that flows, such as water
natural	found in nature and not made by people
orbit	move around a star or planet in a curved path
surface	the outside layer of something
volcanoes	mountains that sometimes erupt and give off very hot melted rock and gases

Index

Solar System Explorers

Titles in This Series

- Earth
- Jupiter
- Mars
- Mercury
- Neptune
- Pluto and Other Dwarf Planets
- Saturn
- Uranus
- Venus

ISBN: 9781534549944

9 781534 549944

KidHaven Publishing

Solar System Explorers
Saturn
Rebekah Banks